In
1935 if you wanted to
read a good book, you needed
either a lot of money or a library card.
Cheap paperbacks were available, but their
poor production generally mirrored the quality
between the covers. One weekend that year,
Allen Lane, Managing Director of The Bodley Head,
having spent the weekend visiting Agatha Christie,
found himself on a platform at Exeter station trying to
find something to read for his journey back to London.
He was appalled by the quality of the material he had to
choose from. Everything that Allen Lane achieved from that
day until his death in 1970 was based on a passionate belief
in the existence of 'a vast reading public for *intelligent*
books at a low price'. The result of his momentous vision
was the birth not only of Penguin, but of the 'paperback
revolution'. Quality writing became available for the price of
a packet of cigarettes, literature became a mass medium
for the first time, a nation of book-borrowers became a
nation of book-buyers – and the very concept of book
publishing was changed for ever. Those founding
principles – of quality and value, with an overarching
belief in the fundamental importance of reading –
have guided everything the company has
done since 1935. Sir Allen Lane's
pioneering spirit is still very much alive
at Penguin in 2005. Here's to
the next 70 years!

MORE THAN A BUSINESS

'We decided it was time to end the almost customary half-hearted manner in which cheap editions were produced – as though the only people who could possibly want cheap editions must belong to a lower order of intelligence. We, however, believed in the existence in this country of a vast reading public for intelligent books at a low price, and staked everything on it'
Sir Allen Lane, 1902–1970

'The Penguin Books are splendid value for sixpence, so splendid that if other publishers had any sense they would combine against them and suppress them'
George Orwell

'More than a business ... a national cultural asset'
Guardian

'When you look at the whole Penguin achievement you know that it constitutes, in action, one of the more democratic successes of our recent social history'
Richard Hoggart

The School Inspector Calls

GERVASE PHINN

PENGUIN BOOKS

PENGUIN BOOKS

Published by the Penguin Group
Penguin Books Ltd, 80 Strand, London WC2R ORL, England
Penguin Group (USA) Inc., 375 Hudson Street, New York, New York 10014, USA
Penguin Group (Canada), 10 Alcorn Avenue, Toronto, Ontario, Canada M4V 3B2
(a division of Pearson Penguin Canada Inc.)
Penguin Ireland, 25 St Stephen's Green, Dublin 2, Ireland
(a division of Penguin Books Ltd)
Penguin Group (Australia), 250 Camberwell Road, Camberwell, Victoria 3124,
Australia (a division of Pearson Australia Group Pty Ltd)
Penguin Books India Pvt Ltd, 11 Community Centre,
Panchsheel Park, New Delhi – 110 017, India
Penguin Group (NZ), cnr Airborne and Rosedale Roads, Albany,
Auckland 1310, New Zealand (a division of Pearson New Zealand Ltd)
Penguin Books (South Africa) (Pty) Ltd, 24 Sturdee Avenue,
Rosebank 2196, South Africa

Penguin Books Ltd, Registered Offices: 80 Strand, London WC2R ORL, England

www.penguin.com

1

The Other Side of the Dale published in Penguin Books 1998
Over Hill and Dale published in Penguin Books 2000
Head Over Heels in the Dale published in Penguin Books 2002
Up and Down in the Dales published in Penguin Books 2004
This selection published as a Pocket Penguin 2005

Copyright © Gervase Phinn, 1998, 2000, 2002, 2004
All rights reserved

The moral right of the author has been asserted

Set in 11/13pt Monotype Dante
Typeset by Palimpsest Book Production Limited
Polmont, Stirlingshire
Printed in England by Clays Ltd, St Ives plc

Dr Gore smiled like a hungry vampire, the sort of thin-lipped, self-satisfied smile of Count Dracula before he sinks his fangs into a helpless victim.

'And how are you, Gervase?' he mouthed softly, showing a glimpse of teeth.

'Oh . . . er . . . very well, thank you, Dr Gore,' I replied, attempting to sound cheerful and relaxed.

'Good, good,' the Chief Education Officer for the County of Yorkshire murmured. He stared for a moment over the top of his small, gold-framed spectacles and then, resting his elbows on the large mahogany desk in front of him, steepled his long fingers and nodded thoughtfully. 'And how have you found your first year with us in Yorkshire?' he asked. His voice was as soft as the summer breeze.

'Oh . . . er . . . very well, thank you, Dr Gore,' I replied for the second time and shifted nervously in the chair. He continued to smile and steeple his long fingers without saying a word. In the embarrassed silence that followed I heard the slow ticking of the clock on the wall, the distant hum of traffic on the High Street and a slight buzzing of a faulty fluorescent light in the outer office. 'I think, well, quite good actually, quite success-ful . . . ' My voice trailed off. I sounded incredibly inar-ticulate for the County Inspector of Schools for English and Drama. 'Not too bad,' I said finally.

'Good, good,' the CEO said almost in a whisper. 'I expect you are wondering why I sent for you so early in the new academic year?' he continued, smiling and steepling.

'Yes, I *was* wondering,' I replied nervously.

The morning had started off so well. I had arrived at the Education Office in Fettlesham that first day of the new term, bright and early and keen to be back at work. A warm September sun had shone in a cloudless sky, the air had been fresh and still, the birds singing and everything had seemed right with the world. Over the summer break, while the schools had been on holiday, I had managed to clear my desk of the mountain of paperwork. I had surveyed the empty desk with a sense of real satisfaction and achievement.

It had been a fascinating first year, occasionally exhausting and frustrating, but for most of the time full of variety and challenge. The colleagues with whom I worked and shared an office had been immensely supportive during my induction into the profession of school inspector. There was Dr Harold Yeats, the Senior Inspector, Sidney Clamp, the unpredictable and larger-than-life Creative and Visual Arts Inspector, and David Pritchard, the small, good-humoured Welshman respon-sible for mathematics, PE and games. We got on well together, and were supported and kept in order by Julie, the inspectors' secretary.

That first year, I had worked alongside teachers in the classroom, organised courses and conferences, directed workshops, run seminars and attended governors' meetings and appointment panels. The most interesting part of the job, however, had involved visiting the small primary schools in the heart of the beautiful Yorkshire Dales, to spend a morning or an afternoon observing lessons, looking at the children's work and reporting on the quality of the teaching and learning.

As I sat at my empty desk, thinking about the quiet, uneventful, stress-free day ahead of me, I heard a clattering on the stairs, telling me that a moment later Julie would totter in on those absurdly high-heeled shoes she was so fond of wearing. In my first year Julie had been invaluable. Not only was she very efficient, good-humoured and extremely comical, she had those qualities often possessed by Yorkshire people – generous to a fault, hard-working but with a blunt nature and a fierce honesty, characteristics which often got her into trouble. With her bright bubbly blonde hair and bright bubbly nature, Julie was a breath of fresh air in the drab and cramped office. That morning she struggled into the room, breathing heavily and loaded down with assorted bags and files. I jumped up to help her.

'I feel like some sort of peripatetic car boot sale!' she cried, dropping her load noisily on the nearest desk. Before I could open my mouth she continued, 'I started off with a handbag and a bit of shopping but collected this little lot on my way up here. As I was passing Committee Room One, Debbie – you know, the big woman with the peroxide hair who always wears those awful pink knitted outfits – asked me to take Mr Pritchard's briefcase which he left there last term. Forget his head if it wasn't screwed on. Anyway, when I got to the Post Room that Derek – you know, the gangly lad with the spectacles and big ears – asked me to pick up the inspectors' mail since I was going that way anyway. Then I had these confidential staffing files pushed into my hands when I reached Personnel. They weigh a ton. I don't know why Dr Yeats didn't pick them up himself. I must have looked like an old pack horse, stumbling along the corridors of County Hall.' She shook her head and breathed out heavily. 'I'm too good-natured by half, that's my trouble. And I've snagged a nail.' She began to rootle about in her hand-bag but continued chattering on without pausing. 'Anyway, how are you?' I attempted a response but without success. 'I had a nail file in here somewhere, I'm sure I did,' she continued. 'I don't know about you, but I could murder a strong cup of coffee.' Without waiting for an answer she disappeared out of the room.

'Good morning, Julie!' I shouted after her, at last getting a word in. I thought of the wonderfully descriptive and rather unkind Yorkshire expression which describes a person like Julie, someone who so enjoys talking about anything and everything that it becomes almost a running commentary: 'She's got a runaway gob – talks and says nowt and she's said nowt when she's done.'

A few minutes later, when I was sorting through my mail, Julie returned with two steaming mugs. I watched as she set one mug down on my desk and cupped her hands around the other.

'You're very quiet today,' she said. 'Is something wrong?'

'Nothing at all, Julie,' I replied amiably, putting my letters into the in-tray on my desk. Then I asked a question which I immediately regretted, for it started her off on another monologue. 'How was your holiday?'

'Don't ask!'

'Not too good then?' I hazarded, looking up and reaching for the coffee.

'Awful! I don't even want to think about it. What was your holiday like?'

'Oh, very restful,' I told her. 'I managed to get away for a few days and –'

Before I could elaborate Julie dived in with her characteristic bluntness. 'And did you see much of that sexy teacher you were taking out?'

'Unfortunately, not a great deal,' I replied smiling and thinking of what Christine's reaction would be to Julie's comment about her.

I had met Christine almost exactly a year earlier when I had visited the infant school where she was the Headteacher. She had appeared like some vision and I had been bowled over by those large blue eyes, warm smile, fair complexion and soft mass of golden hair. After a long period spent summoning up the courage, and with constant nagging from my colleagues in the office, I had asked her out. We had been to the theatre and the cinema, to a concert and various school events and as each day passed I felt sure I was falling in love with her. This term I was determined I was going to see a whole lot more of her.

'So what's happening with you two then?' asked Julie. She was not one to beat about the bush.

'What do you mean, what's happening?'

'Well, are you getting it together? Is it serious?'

'I'm not sure . . .' I started.

Julie folded her arms and pulled a face. 'Typical of men that – "I'm not sure." Indecisive!'

I decided to change the subject. 'Am I the only one in the office this morning?'

'It's always the woman who has to make the decisions. What did you say?'

'I asked if I was the only one in the office this morning.'

'Just you. Mr Clamp's planning his art course, Mr Pritchard's meeting with the newly qualified teachers and Dr Yeats is at a conference. There's not much mail either, by the look of it.'

'So,' I said happily, 'it looks like a quiet start to the term.'

'Not necessarily,' said Julie. 'Mrs Savage phoned last Friday.' At this point her lip curled like a rabid dog and her voice became hard-edged. 'She wondered where you were. I said, "People do take holidays, you know." If she'd have bothered to look at those wretched inspectors' engagement sheets I have to send over to Admin. every week, she'd have seen that you were on leave. She just likes the sound of her own voice and it's not her real voice anyway. She puts it on. I don't know who she thinks she's trying to impress.'

I began to chuckle and shake my head. 'You've really got it in for Mrs Savage, Julie, and no mistake. She's not that bad.'

'She's *unbearable*. "Ho," says she, "well tell Mr Phinn, when he returns on Monday, thet Dr Gore wishes to see him in his room has a metter of hurgency at nine hey hem prompt." Made you sound like a naughty schoolboy. Then she slams the phone down with no trace of a "please" or a "thank you".' Julie's face screwed up as if she had chronic indigestion.

Mrs Savage, the CEO's personal assistant, was not the most popular of people in our office, nor was she the easiest woman to get on with. She had a formidable reputation with a sharp tongue and a stare that could curdle milk; she definitely was not a person with whom to cross swords.

'And speaking of getting under people's skin,' said Julie, 'I reckon she's had her face done.'

'Who?' I asked.

'Mrs Savage. When I saw her last week in the staff canteen I didn't recognise her. Her skin's been stretched right back off her face. She looks as if she's walking through a wind tunnel. All those wrinkles have disappeared. Those two pouches under her chin have gone as well.'

'I don't remember her having pouches.'

'Of course you do! She looked like a gerbil with

mumps. And I think she's had that rhinosuction because she looks a lot thinner as well.'

'Liposuction,' I corrected.

'She's that thick-skinned, I think I was right first time. She gave me such a glare. I tell you, if looks could maim, I'd be on crutches.'

'And she said Dr Gore wanted to see me?'

'She's unbearable, that woman,' said Julie with venom, 'you would think –'

'Julie!' I snapped. 'Did Mrs Savage say that Dr Gore wanted to see me?'

'At nine o'clock prompt. That's what Lady High and Mighty said.'

'I wonder what it's about?'

'She puts on that posh accent and that hoity-toity manner but it doesn't fool me. Marlene on the switchboard remembers her when she started as an office junior. That's when her hair colour was natural. She had a voice as broad as a barn door and was croaky as a frog with laryngitis. Then she went through all those husbands like a dose of salts and was promoted far beyond her capabilities and she now speaks as if she's got a potato in her mouth.'

'I think the expression is "a plum in her mouth".'

'With a mouth like hers, it's definitely a potato. When I think of the times –'

'Did she say what Dr Gore wanted?' I interrupted. I was feeling rather uneasy about this interview with the CEO so early on in the term. A small cold dread was settling into the pit of my stomach.

'No, I never gave her the chance. I keep all conversations with that woman as short as possible. But,' Julie said, with a mischievous glint in her eye, 'it could be one of his little jobs.'

'Oh no!' I exclaimed. 'Not one of his little jobs! Please don't let it be one of his little jobs!' I was well acquainted with Dr Gore's little jobs, having been given several in my first year – and they were never 'little' jobs. There had been the county-wide reading survey and the full audit of secondary school libraries followed by a detailed report to the Education Committee. There had been the investigation into the teaching of spelling, the production of a series of guideline documents for teachers, and the organising of the visit of the Minister of Education. All this was extra work on the top of the courses, inspections and report writing. I prayed it was not one of Dr Gore's little jobs.

Dr Gore continued to smile like a hungry vampire as he leaned forward in his chair. He peered over his glasses, his eyes glinting like chips of glass. 'Well, Gervase,' he murmured, stroking his brow with a long finger. I just knew what he was going to say. He was going to say, 'I have a little job for you.'

'I have a little job for you,' he said.

Ten minutes later Julie was waiting for me at the top of the stairs. 'Well?'

'One guess.'

'A little job?'

'Right first time.'

'I'll put the coffee on.'

I followed her into the office. 'Actually, it's not too bad,' I said cheerfully, rattling the change in my trouser pocket. 'Dr Gore's asked me to organise a visit of one of Her Majesty's Inspectors for later this term. He wants to look at some schools as part of a national information gathering exercise on literacy standards. I just have to nominate a number of schools and arrange things, nothing massively demanding in that. I can ring round the schools this morning and get a letter off to the Ministry. There's not much else for me to do today. The only fly in the ointment is having to liaise with Mrs Savage.'

Julie pulled the screwed-up face again and clattered out of the office. 'Forget the coffee,' she said, 'I'll get the brandy.'

One bright morning a week later I was looking casually through my post when I came on an exceedingly official-looking envelope. On the back there was a large royal crest with a rampant lion and a rearing unicorn, the two topped with a crown. The letter inside had a black embossed heading – The Ministry of Education – and ended with a large flourish of a signature. I recognised the name: Miss W. de la Mare.

Miss de la Mare, Her Majesty's Principal Divisional Inspector of Schools, had contacted me the previous year when I had been given the 'little job' of arranging the visit of the Minister of Education. She had barked down the telephone at Julie that she had wanted to speak to me to discuss the visit and then had promptly hung up. Julie had told me that the speaker 'was like a grizzly bear with toothache' and had given a name that sounded like 'Deadly Stare'. In the event Miss de la Mare's bark was far worse than her bite. In the letter I had now, she requested that I arrange a series of visits to schools 'which demonstrate good practice in the teaching of reading and writing' and which 'show good breadth, balance and continuity in the curriculum'. She was particularly interested in poetry.

I knew just the school for her to visit: Backwatersthwaite Primary, the very first school I had called at when I had started in my new career as an inspector a year earlier.

2

At long last, after a two-hour search up and down the dale, along muddy twisting roads, across narrow stone bridges, up dirt tracks, past swirling rivers and dribbling streams, and through countless villages in an increasingly desperate search, I had eventually arrived at my destination. At the sight of the highly-polished brass plate on the door bearing the words BACKWATERSTHWAITE SCHOOL, I heaved a great sigh of relief and felt that sort of pioneering triumph that Christopher Columbus, Captain Cook and Scott of the Antarctic must have felt on arriving at their destinations after their difficult journeys.

I had seen no school sign, no playground, nothing that

would identify the austere building as an educational institution. The tall and somewhat gaunt edifice, set deep in the dark valley, looked like any other large, sturdy Yorkshire country house and I had already unknowingly driven past it during my vain attempt to discover the elusive school. Beneath the slate roof, grey and edged with pale purple lichen, tall leaded windows faced the ever-watchful fields. From the grey and white limestone walls, gillyflowers and tiny ferns peeped, and a little beck trickled alongside. At long last I had arrived and I made my way to the heavy oak door. I lifted the great grey iron knocker in the shape of a ram's head and let it fall with a heavy echoing thud.

I had arrived at Upperwatersthwaite much earlier in the afternoon assuming, quite foolishly, that it was somewhere near Backwatersthwaite. As soon as I stepped through the door of the busy little village post office to ask for directions, all conversation ceased and every suspicious eye was directed my way.

'I wonder if you could direct me to Backwatersthwaite?' I asked cheerfully. 'I seem to have got myself well and truly lost.' The countenance of one large woman underwent a rapid transformation. She beamed widely and two great dimples appeared on her round rosy cheeks. She gave a long, audible sigh before she replied.

'Oh, is that all?' she said. 'I thowt for a minute you were here for summat else.' I suppose she had imagined me to be some sort of post office investigator, tax inspector or auditor and, hearing that I was not there to check the books, visibly relaxed. 'Ee, you're miles away from Backwatersthwaite, love,' she chuckled. 'You want t'other side of t'dale.' Then followed a series of detailed instructions on how to get to Backwatersthwaite, punctuated periodically by the other customers in the post office. The journey, described in seemingly endless detail, involved a veritable expedition that would take me via Brigg Rock and Hopton Crags, past Woppat's Farm and then the Bull and Heifer Inn at Lowerwatersthwaite, next through Bishopwatersthwaite, Chapelwatersthwaite, and along Stoneybrow Rise, and over Saddleside Edge.

'Then tha' best ask ageean,' the postmistress concluded. Her customers nodded in agreement. I thanked her, looked at my watch and made hastily for the door. 'And tha wants to slow down, love!' she shouted after me. 'It'll still be theer when thy arrives – it's not goin' anyweer.' Her words were accompanied by several grunts from the others.

Having negotiated Brigg Rock and passed by Hopton Crags at great speed with no sign of Woppat's Farm, I whizzed through a couple of small villages and arrived at Chapelwatersthwaite. The hamlet was a cluster of barns and cottages, a tall redbrick primitive Methodist chapel and one small country inn: the Marrick Arms. In the centre of the village the road forked and I stopped the car at the side of the road for the umpteenth time that day to find my bearings. I cursed myself for forgetting to bring a map with me. I had been told at the office that the school was easy to find: just head down the dale, follow the signs and you cannot miss it. I decided on the wider of the two roads, which twisted and turned for half a mile, then narrowed to a single track, then became a dirt track and finally came to a dead end at a gate on which was printed CRABTREE FARM – PRIVATE PROPERTY. I reversed angrily until I could find a gate to turn in, and made my way back to the Marrick Arms. An old ancient was standing outside the inn, holding an equally ancient spaniel on a piece of binder twine. I wound down the car window wearily to ask him for directions.

'Backwatersthwaite? What's tha' goin' up to Backwatersthwaite fer? There's nowt theer.' I explained that I had an appointment at the school. 'Scoil?' he repeated. 'Scoil! Nay, lad, they closed t'scoil in nineteen fotty!' I assured him that I had an appointment with the headteacher of the school that very afternoon and that he would be expecting me about now.

The old man regarded me with a grave expression. 'Well I nivver did. They've gone an oppened it up ageean. There must be another family up t'dale.'

I finally extracted directions from him and set off once more. And so it was that half an hour later I was standing outside the gaunt, grey building, waiting for someone to answer my thump with the ram's head knocker. I heard slow footsteps and a few seconds later the door was opened by a lean, stooping man with grey frizzy hair like a mass of wire-wool and a most pallid complexion. The figure looked as if he had survived the Electric Chair.

'Yes?'

'Mr Lapping?'

'Yes.'

'I think you were expecting me.'

'Was I?'

'Yes, I wrote you a letter.'

'Did you?'

'Yes. I said I would be calling this afternoon.'

'Did you?'

'Yes, I did!' I replied in an exasperated voice and getting rather tired of this verbal badinage. 'My name is Phinn.'

'Are you the man who does the guttering repairs?'

'No, I am not!' I replied sharply. 'I am the man who does the school inspections.'

'Oh.'

'I'm the newly-appointed County Inspector of Schools for this area.'

'Are you indeed?'

'And I am making a number of initial visits to all the schools in this part of the county. Yours is one of the first schools I have on my list.'

'Is it indeed? I am most flattered.'

'Do you not remember, Mr Lapping? I wrote earlier last week saying I would be calling today?'

The tall figure scratched the growth of frizzy hair, but remained in the doorway, showing no sign of letting me enter the building. 'I do remember receiving a letter now I come to think of it,' he said. 'Official looking, in a brown envelope. Yes, I believe I did receive something of the sort. Actually, I've been so very busy that I have not got round to dealing with all the mail. I'm a *teaching* headteacher, you see, and I have to deal with letters and such when I can.' Then he glanced at his watch. 'But you are a little late for visiting, Mr Flynn. The children go home at three thirty and it's getting on for half past four.'

'Yes, I am sorry about the delay. I had some difficulty finding the school.'

'Most people do,' replied the Headteacher, smiling and nodding sagely.

'Never mind,' I shrugged. 'It was you I wished to speak to, Mr Lapping. Perhaps now that I know how to get here, I could arrange a further visit to see the children at work?' He still made no move to welcome me inside. 'Do you think I might come in?'

'Yes, yes, of course,' he said with sudden eagerness. 'How very remiss of me, keeping you standing on the doorstep. Do, do come in, Mr Flynn.'

I entered a large, bright classroom. Children's paintings, collages and poems covered the walls, while various savage-looking stuffed animals glared down from the shelves.

'We don't get many visitors up here once the summer holidays are over. I must admit I was quite surprised to see you at the door. And as for coming to see the children at work,' he continued amiably, 'that would be very nice, very nice indeed. We always enjoy visitors. Now I feel sure you would enjoy a cup of tea before you head off back down the dale.'

'Yes, please,' I replied. 'But I don't intend to leave just yet. I would like to examine the school documentation to put me in the picture before I go.'

'School documentation?' He looked at me quizzically.

'Yes, reading test results, mathematics scores, school prospectus, the parents' brochure, curriculum policies, guidelines and, of course, your School Development Plan.'

'My *what*?' he asked.

'Your School Development Plan. The document which sets out your aims, objectives, targets and forward planning initiatives.'

'I haven't got one.' He gave a wan smile.

'Oh, I see,' I murmured. 'Well, every school should have one.'

'I don't think I'd recognise one if it flew in through the window and that's the truth of it, Mr Flynn.'

'It's Phinn actually,' I said.

'You better tell me about this School Development Plan of yours over that cup of tea I promised to make.'

So we sat in the schoolroom by a window through which we looked upon great dark hills which rose all around and I outlined what the writing of a School Development Plan involved.

When I had finished the schoolmaster sighed. 'You know, Mr Phinn, I've been a teacher in this school for near on forty years. I came here as a boy, taught all the children's parents and went to school with most of their grandparents. This school is a part of me. I live and breathe it. Look around. Outside is one of the most magnificent views in the world. Inside is a richness and a range and quality of work which speaks for itself. Every child in this school can read and write well, every child knows his or her tables, can paint and dance and sing and they all get on as you'll see on your next visit.' As I looked around me I knew these were no idle boasts. 'I would never leave this place,' he continued. 'When I visit the town I see all the people rushing about, with appointments to keep, no time to look at the fells or the colours in the sky.' He paused. 'You town dwellers have a lot to learn about us country folk. It's a different way of life. It took fifty years for the Reformation to reach us up here in the dale, Mr Phinn. I'll do my best, of course, but I reckon it'll be a while before you get your School Development Plan.'

I returned a month later. The drive along the cold grey roads was more leisurely and thoughtful. I skirted Brigg Rock and Hopton Crags, sheer and black and surrounded by tall ancient trees, through a deserted Chapel-watersthwaite and along Stoneybrow Rise where the banks were peppered with a dusting of hoarfrost, over the grim and silent Saddleside Edge to discover again the small school. It stood grey and secure in the deep valley where a wide unhurried river, brown with recent rain, flowed gently beneath the arches of the slender bridge.

The morning I spent with the children was memorable. They sat open-mouthed as their teacher read a story in a soft and captivating voice, they answered questions with enthusiasm and unusual perception, and they wrote the most moving and vivid poetry. Before I left, Daniel, a small nine-year-old with wide, unblinking eyes and hair as thick and bright as the bracken that covered the distant hills, approached me.

'Are thar t'scoil inspector?' he asked, his small face creasing into a serious expression.

'Yes,' I replied, 'I am.'

'Well, can I tell thee summat?'

'Of course.'

'I just wanted to tell you thee he's all reight, is Mester Lapping. He's a reight good teacher, tha knaws.' I looked into the innocent eyes and smiled. 'Aren't tha' goin' to write it down in tha' big black book?' he continued. 'It's just that tha' might forget.'

'No,' I replied gently, watching the tall, stooping, rather eccentric figure who moved amongst his pupils with his calm, patient and gentle manner. 'I won't forget.'

3

I replied promptly to the letter from the Ministry of Education suggesting five schools for Miss de la Mare to visit and offering to accompany her to Backwatersthwaite. I certainly did not want her to spend half the day, as I had done, travelling backwards and forwards through the dale in search of the elusive school.

A couple of days later a second rather sharp-sounding letter arrived from the Ministry informing me that Miss de la Mare was grateful for the list of suitable schools and for my offer to accompany her on one of the visits, but she would prefer to go alone. I immediately telephoned the headteachers at the chosen schools forewarning them of the HMI's visitation.

'Well, thank you very much,' sighed George Lapping down the line. 'Thank you very much indeed. I know now who my friends really are.' I could guess from the tone of his voice that he was secretly pleased but he made the pretence of displeasure. 'I have attempted, Gervase, over the many years I have been a teacher and headteacher in this vast and beautiful county, to avoid the attentions of school inspectors. My school is isolated, difficult to find and subtly disguised to resemble the façade of a private house. I have kept my head down, got on with my teaching and not done too bad a job, even if I say so myself. Now, with your recent arrival in the county, Backwatersthwaite has been put firmly on the map. I guess there will be coaches creeping up the dale full of educationalists and researchers, school parties even. Now I have an HMI putting me under the microscope.'

'You should be very flattered that I recommended your school, George,' I replied. 'It's a mark of the excellent work which your pupils achieve. As Shakespeare would have it, "Some are born great, some achieve greatness and some have greatness thrust upon them."'

'But I have an *HMI* thrust upon me! Well, I just hope he has the same difficulty finding the school as you did when you first came here, Gervase. I can't be doing with visitors. They interrupt my teaching routine with all their questions. Anyway, when is this visit likely to take place?'

'Oh, some time this term,' I replied. 'I'm not exactly sure, but you'll be given good warning. By the way, George –' I was about to tell him that the HMI in question would be a woman but he cut me off.

'And I do not intend putting on anything special for him. He'll just have to take us as he finds us. Anyway, if he intends coming out in November or December, he had better reconsider. It's like Tibet up here in the winter.'

I tried again to explain that the HMI intending to visit him was not a man but Miss de la Mare, and quite a forceful character at that, but he never gave me the chance. 'I shall have to go. Break is over and there's children to teach. I'll let you know how I get on.' With that the line went dead.

As soon as I had replaced the receiver, however, the telephone rang. I snatched it up.

'George,' I said, assuming it would be the previous speaker, 'I meant to say that the HMI –'

The voice which replied was coldly formal. 'This is Mrs Savage.' I jumped as if someone had poured a bucket of cold water down my back. 'Is that Mr Phinn?'

'Yes, yes, Mrs Savage,' I said. 'I thought you were someone else.'

'Mr Phinn,' she said primly, 'it was my understanding that you and I were going to liaise?'

'Going to what?' I asked.

'Liaise,' she repeated. 'I understood from Dr Gore that we were going to liaise over the visit of the HMI.'

'Oh yes, he did sort of mention something about that.'

'Mr Phinn, Dr Gore does not sort of mention something. Dr Gore is always very specific and precise and he clearly informed me that you were going to get in touch to liaise about this intended visit of the HMI. I was to deal with all the administrative arrangements.'

'I see,' I said lamely.

'Clearly you do not see, Mr Phinn.'

'I'm sorry?'

'I have not heard a thing,' she said tartly. When I did not respond she continued. 'I did telephone earlier in the week but your secretary – who is not the easiest person to deal with, I have to say – was in rather a tetchy mood. Something had obviously got under her skin that morning.' At the mention of 'skin' and Julie I recalled the earlier conversation about Mrs Savage's plastic surgery. I winced and held my breath to keep from laughing.

'Are you still there?' came the strident voice down the line.

'Yes, yes, I am.'

'And then, this morning, as I was dealing with Dr Gore's correspondence, I came across a letter from the Ministry of Education informing him that the visits have already been arranged.'

'The thing is, it was a pretty simple task, Mrs Savage,' I said. 'I saw no reason to bother you about it.'

I heard a sort of clucking noise down the telephone. 'So I take it that you have contacted the schools, arranged the visits and organised everything else as well?' I could imagine the stiffening of the shoulders, the hawk-like countenance and the flashing eyes.

'Yes, I have.'

'I see. Well perhaps you will do me the courtesy, next time we are asked to liaise, of letting me know that you intend to do it all yourself.'

'As I said, Mrs Savage, it was not an onerous task and –'

'I shall, of course, be informing Dr Gore of the situation. I expect you have sent him all the details?'

'It is in draft now,' I said, pulling a clean pad of paper towards me, 'and he will have it in the morning.'

There was a pause followed by the clucking noise again. 'Well, there seems little more to say.' With that, she replaced the receiver.

I took a deep, deep breath, turned to the window and exhaled noisily. The morning had started off promisingly, but how things could change in a matter of hours, I thought to myself.

4

One afternoon some weeks later, on my way back from collecting some guideline documents from the Print Room, I bumped into George Lapping in a corridor in County Hall.

'Hello,' he said laconically.

'What are you doing at County Hall, George?' I asked. 'I thought you rarely ventured out of Backwaters-thwaite.'

'I've been dragooned,' he said.

'Pardon?'

'Enlisted, press-ganged, selected to sit on one of these advisory committees. I got the sort of invitation you couldn't refuse from the CEO. It's on "Key Skills". Now what do I know about key skills? You're responsible, of course, for putting me in the spotlight and encouraging that HMI to visit me. I knew it would happen.'

'I meant to give you a ring about the HMI. She's been then, has she?'

'Oh, she's been all right,' he replied with a wry chuckle.

'Have you got a minute, George?' I asked him. 'I would be glad if you could fill me in.'

Five minutes later, over a cup of tea, George was giving me a blow-by-blow account of the visitation of Miss Winifred de la Mare, HMI.

'For a start,' began George, 'I didn't remember receiving this letter which she said she sent, saying when she would be coming, so it was a real shock when she arrived on my doorstep. I was walking up the path to the school one morning just before half past eight and, as I always do, I paused to admire that lovely view. Anyway, as I approached the entrance, a huge brown creature jumped out at me. It gave me the shock of my life. I thought at first it was a grizzly bear. When I had calmed down a bit, I realised it was, in fact, a large woman in thick brown tweeds, heavy brogues and a hat in the shape of a flowerpot.

'"You were expecting me!" she snaps.

'"Was I?" I replied.

'"Yes!" says she.

'"Oh!" says I.

'"I wrote you a letter," says she.

'"Did you?" says I.

'"It was very important," says she.

'"Was it?" says I.

'"Official!" says she. "In a large brown envelope."

'"Really?" says I.

'"The name is de la Mare," says she. "Do you not remember?"

'"Can't say as I do," says I.'

As George recounted his meeting with the HMI, it brought back memories of my first meeting with him and the verbal ping-pong we had played for a good few minutes before he had discovered that I was not the man to fix the guttering but a school inspector. I thought to myself that he might have learnt something from that experience. He clearly had not.

'So then what happened?' I asked.

'I told her that I received lots of letters but, because I was a teaching head, I had to deal with correspondence when I could find the time. She followed me into the school, peering around her as if it were a museum, declined a cup of tea, plonked herself down on my chair, took the flowerpot off her head and got out this thick wadge of paper from her big black bag.

'"I'm ready to commence," says she.

'"Are you?" says I.

'"I am," says she.

'I pointed out to her that the children had not yet arrived so there was not much point in "commencing" anything, but at nine o'clock after the register she could get started. I asked her if she wanted to begin with the infants and work up or with the juniors and work down.

'"I wish to start with you, Mr Lapping," she says, fixing me with those gimlet eyes of hers. "I want to discuss the teaching of spelling, grammar and punctuation, approaches to poetry, drama and story writing, standards of literacy, the handwriting policy, reading in the early years and the level of comprehension." It was like an educational shopping list.

'"Hang on, Miss Mare," I says.

'"De la," says she, "it's de la Mare."'

I shut my eyes and groaned inwardly – I could guess what was coming.

'"OK, Della," I says.' (Bingo!) '"I don't have all that information at my fingertips, you know."

'"Well, don't you think you ought to, Mr Lapping?" says she.

'I tried to explain to her that document after document arrived at the school like the plagues of Egypt, that I'd got a broken boiler, faulty pipes, toilets which wouldn't flush, a leaking roof, three children with chicken pox and a member of staff suffering from stress who, having just returned from one of Mr Clamp's art courses, was ready to chuck herself down a pothole on Hopton Crags.

'"Nevertheless, Mr Lapping," says she, "it would be helpful to have some information on all these matters."

'"Well, it's a new one to me," says I. "It's the first time in nearly forty years of teaching that the nit nurse has wanted that sort of information from me."'

I winced. 'Oh heavens! You thought she was the school nurse?'

'Well, of course I did. How was I to know she was one of these HMIs? I've only ever met one in the whole of my career and he was an old man in a suit, with a hangdog expression. I was certainly not expecting a strapping great woman in tweeds. I mean, she looked like the nit nurse.'

'How did she react?' I hardly dared ask.

'She stared at me for a moment with a sort of glazed expression and then she smiled. "Let's start again, Mr Lapping," she said. "My name is Winifred de la Mare, HMI."

'We got on like a house on fire after that, particularly when she had met the children and read their poetry and stories. She liked what she saw so much she's coming back in the spring.'

'I really am delighted,' I said. 'Maybe I could come out to meet her when she returns?'

'Oh, you'll be meeting her all right, Gervase,' George Lapping replied. 'She was very interested in the creative writing we were doing, said it was very innovative, so I told her I got the ideas from one of your literacy courses and I suggested that she might care to join you on the next one you direct. Those little eyes of hers lit up at the thought. She said it was an excellent suggestion and that she will, no doubt, be getting in touch with you.'

'Well, thank you very much,' I replied sourly.

'You should be very flattered,' he told me, with a mischievous ring in his voice. 'It's a mark of the excellent in-service you provide that I have recommended you.' With that, he made for the door, waved his hand dramatically and departed with the words: "'Some are born great, some achieve greatness and some have greatness thrust upon them.'"

5

I arrived at the Education Office feeling on top of the world.

'You're looking pretty chipper, Gervase,' remarked Sidney as I entered the room, humming.

'I am feeling pretty chipper actually, Sidney,' I replied cheerfully.

'I take it you have made all your school visits, and written all your reports?' remarked David, looking up from his papers and removing his spectacles.

'Yes, things have gone well, thank you, David.'

'There's a definite spring in your step,' continued Sidney, 'an eagerness in your eye and a rather smug little smile playing about your lips. I could hear you whistling up the stairs like a blackbird with the early morning worm.'

'It would hardly be whistling, this blackbird of yours,' observed David, putting down his pen, 'if it had a beak full of worms.'

'Oh, don't be so pedantic,' retorted Sidney. 'I didn't say the blackbird had the worm in its beak, did I?'

'Well, where would it have the worm then, if it's not in its beak – tucked under its wing? In a shopping basket?'

'Look, the worm is immaterial –' began Sidney.

'Is this conversation leading anywhere?' I interrupted.

Sidney ignored me. 'What I meant, David, is that Gervase looks like the cat that has caught the mouse. Now is that comparison acceptable to you?'

'When you two have quite finished –' I attempted to get a word in but had no success.

'Not really,' continued David. 'That's just a boring cliché.'

'Now I wonder why our young colleague here is looking so very pleased with himself this bright morning?' remarked Sidney, ignoring David and swivelling around on his chair to face me. '

'Possibly because today is Children's Reading Day,' I suggested, 'and for most of the time I shall be doing what I really enjoy – touring schools encouraging children to read.'

'Or could it, by any chance, be because you are about to see the woman of your dreams, the Venus of Fettlesham, the Aphrodite of the education world, the delectable Miss Christine Bentley of Winnery Nook Nursery and Infant School?'

'How do you know I am visiting Winnery Nook this morning?'

'You can't keep anything from me, dear boy. Actually, Julie mentioned that you had the visit on your engagement sheet for this week. Now do tell us, how are things going with that Nordic beauty of yours?'

Before I could reply, David looked up again from his

papers. 'She's a real cracker, is that Miss Bentley,' he said. 'As my grandfather – he was the one who had the sheep farm near Builth Wells – used to say, "*Fyddai hi yn berffaith petai hi yn Gymraes.*".

'I could not have expressed it better myself,' remarked Sidney. 'And what in heaven's name does that mouthful of gutteral gibberish mean? Whenever you start spouting Welsh I always think you're choking on a bone.'

'It means, "If she were Welsh, she'd be perfect"!' replied David. 'And I'll tell you this. If I was fancy-free, with a bit more hair on my head and less of a spare tyre around the tummy, I'd be after her like a rat up a drainpipe.'

'"Like a rat up a drainpipe"!' Sidney repeated, snorting. 'What a wonderful way with words you Welsh have! "Like a rat up a drainpipe." Most original and descriptive. I don't know how you have the brass neck to criticise my choice of words when you use that sort of hackneyed expression.'

I had begun to sort through the papers on my desk to check that there was nothing urgent to deal with, trying not to get involved in the endless badinage between Sidney and David. It was impossible, however, not to listen. They were like a comedy duo. One would set off on a line of thought and then the other would respond with a witticism or a clever riposte, each trying to outdo the other.

After a moment's silence, when I thought my two colleagues had returned to their work, Sidney jumped up from his desk, hurried over to where I was standing, put his arm around my shoulder and looked at me with an intense expression upon his face and a gleam in his eye.

'What is it?' I asked.

'Now then, Gervase, you have been particularly elusive when a certain young enchantress is mentioned. How are things going with you and the delightful Headteacher of Winnery Nook?'

'Oh, all right,' I replied, shuffling my papers.

'Another master wordsmith. "Oh, all right",' Sidney snorted again. 'Ever the master of understatement. You are supposed to be an inspector for English, for goodness sake. Can't you do better than "Oh, all right"? What about splendid, fantastic, magnificent, marvellous, amazing, incredible, miraculous, phenomenal, spectacular –'

'All right! All right! Things are going pretty well. I just don't want to tempt fate.'

'So we can assume that you are, in Harold's quaintly old-fashioned words, "walking out" with Miss Bentley, or in Julie's more down-to-earth description "cooartin" and that wedding bells will soon be in the air?'

'No, you certainly cannot assume any such thing. I have taken her out a few times. There's nothing serious at the moment.' I was feeling rather embarrassed and irritated by the way the conversation was going. 'Have you completed this form on school resources yet?' I asked, holding up a yellow sheet of paper, endeavouring to change the subject.

'Oh, you won't get out of answering quite so easily as that,' Sidney told me, plucking the paper from my hand and returning it to the pile on my desk. 'Now do tell. Are things developing satisfactorily in that direction?'

'Look, Sidney,' I groaned, 'I would rather not talk about it. It's gone eight thirty and I have to be in a school in fifteen minutes.'

'Well, you want to go for it, Gervase,' remarked David, leaving his desk to join us. 'You are only young once. And as my grandfather used to say –'

'Oh dear, here we go,' sighed Sidney. 'Another dose of Welsh wisdom.'

'"Live for the moment, for time runs away like the wild horses in the wind." Very imaginative, was my old grandfather. He had a very poetical turn of phrase. But now, about Miss Bentley –'

As the conversation was fast developing into an in-depth analysis of my love life, I decided to leave. Snatching up my mail, I crammed it into my briefcase and headed for the door, nearly knocking Julie over in the process as she entered with three mugs of coffee.

'Somebody's in a hurry!' she exclaimed. 'Rushing around like a rabbit with the runs.'

'Look,' I said quietly but deliberately, and address-ing all three of my companions, 'this morning I have been compared to a blackbird with a beak full of worms, a cat that has got the mouse, a rat up a drain-pipe, a horse in the wind and now a rabbit with the runs. Personally, I feel like a fox pursued by the hounds. I would be very pleased if you left me and my love life alone! And so that no one is in any doubt where I am going, I am off to Winnery Book School for Nook Day, I mean Winnery Nook for Book Day, to see Christine,

I mean Miss Bentley, purely, I may add, in my professional capacity.'

'Of course you are!' they all chorused loudly.

There was a witch waiting for me outside the school. The hideous creature had long knotted black hair that cascaded from beneath a pointed hat, a pale green-tinged face and a crimson slit of a mouth, and she was shrouded in a flowing black cape. As I approached, the red-rimmed eyes fixed me with a glare and a long white-fingered hand with sharp red nails reached out like the talon of some great bird of prey and beckoned. The ghastly crone smiled widely to reveal a mouthful of blackened teeth.

'Hello, Gervase,' she crooned, 'how nice to see you.'

Before me stood the woman I was sure I loved. Beneath the green and red make-up, the tangle of hair and the cloak of black was Miss Christine Bentley, Headteacher of Winnery Nook Nursery and Infant School. She had asked me to visit the school as part of the Children's Reading Day celebrations, to take the school assembly, talk to the children about stories and reading, and judge the competition for the best fancy-dressed characters out of literature. I had looked forward immensely to seeing Christine again and, even dressed as a witch, thought she looked wonderful.

'I thought you were dressing up for Children's Reading Day,' I teased.

'Cheeky thing!' she exclaimed. 'You had better come in. And any more clever comments of that kind and I'll put a spell on you.'

But Christine had already put a spell on me. She had captivated and charmed me, if only she knew it. I walked with her down the school corridor past excited, chattering children dressed as all sorts of characters, fussing parents who were putting the final touches to their children's outfits, and teachers in costume attempting to organise things.

We arrived at the main hall and were surrounded by a knot of colourful little characters, all excited to show themselves off to the headteacher. 'I must welcome the parents and children, Gervase, so if you would like to wait in the staff room, I'll see you in a moment,' she said. 'Make yourself a cup of coffee if you like. Oh, by the way, you'll find the Chairman of Governors in there. She'll be judging the competition with you.'

In the small staff room I found a large, elderly woman with hands on hips and legs planted well apart, staring intently out of the window at the view. She had really gone to town on her costume and was dressed in a wonderfully bizarre outfit. The heavy, old-fashioned suit was a mustard yellow with red and green checks and was as shapeless as a sack of potatoes. The thick stockings were dark red, and her feet were thrust into little leopard-skin patterned boots. To complete the effect, she wore a wide-brimmed red hat sporting two long pheasant feathers, held in place by a silver brooch in the shape of a stag's head. She held a battered old handbag and an ancient umbrella with a swan's head handle. She looked magnificently outlandish.

The multicoloured figure, like some overfed, exotic

bird, turned full circle when she heard me enter. 'Mornin'!' she snapped.

'Good morning,' I replied. 'You really do look the part.'

She stared at me, perplexed. 'Do I?'

'Yes, indeed. Are you Miss Marple?'

'I beg your pardon, young man?'

'Miss Marple?'

'No, I'm not. I'm Sybil Arkwright, Chairman of Governors.'

'But who are you dressed as? Are you not Agatha Christie's sleuth, Miss Marple?'

'Why do you keep going on about Miss Marple? I've already told you, my name is Mrs Arkwright.'

'Yes, but what character are you supposed to be? Are you Mary Poppins?'

'Character? What are you blathering on about? I've not come as any character.' It then dawned upon me that she was wearing her usual apparel. 'I always dress like this.' I urgently wanted the ground to open and swallow me up.

'Of course.' I held out my hand which she shook charily. 'It's my feeble attempt at humour. I'm Gervase Phinn, school inspector, here to judge the competition with you.'

'Pleased to meet you, I'm sure,' said Mrs Arkwright, grimacing and eyeing me suspiciously.

After a short and rather strained conversation, I extricated myself from the company of the colourful Chairman of Governors and went in search of Christine.

I found her in the small reading area of the school. The Wicked Witch of the West was sitting in the corner with her arm around a small boy who was crying piteously. His little body was shaking uncontrollably and great tears streamed down his round red face. Christine held him close with a claw-like hand and tried to comfort him. The child was dressed in twisted yellow tights over which he wore a pair of close-fitting, electric-blue underpants. He had on a baggy white T-shirt with SUPAMAN written incorrectly across the front in large, shaky letters.

'Well, *I* don't think you look a prat, Gavin,' said the witch.

'I do, miss, I do,' whimpered Superman. 'Everyone says I look a prat.'

Christine caught sight of me peering through the bookcases. 'Well, look who's here!' she cried, beckoning me over. 'It's Mr Phinn.' Superman looked up and stifled his sobbing for a moment. He wiped away his tears with a grubby little fist, leaving long streaks across his cheeks, and stared sorrowfully in my direction. 'Now, Mr Phinn is a very important visitor, Gavin, and knows everything about everything because he's an inspector.' The child sniffed loudly and wiped his nose on his hand. 'Do you know what an inspector does?'

The child nodded pathetically before answering. 'He checks bus tickets.'

Christine stifled a laugh before telling the child that I was a school inspector and something of an expert on costumes. 'Shall we ask Mr Phinn what he thinks about your outfit, Gavin?' The child sniffed loudly, wiped his nose again and nodded. 'Well, Mr Phinn,' said Christine, 'do you think Gavin looks a prat?'

'I certainly do not think he looks a prat!' I exclaimed dramatically.

The little boy started to weep and wail again. 'I do! I do! I know I do. Everybody says I do!'

'And I have in my pocket a special piece of paper which says you do not look a prat.' I reached in my jacket, produced a visiting card and wrote on it: 'Superman does not look a prat.'

The little boy took it from me, scrutinised it for a moment and asked: 'Is that what it says?'

'It does,' I replied.

He tucked the card down the back of his electric-blue underpants, sniffed noisily and scurried off.

Christine came over and put her hand on my arm. 'That was sweet,' she said. 'Now let's see how you fare taking the school assembly.'

The infants by this time had gathered in the hall and were sitting cross-legged in their resplendent costumes, facing the front.

'Good morning, children,' said Christine brightly.

'Good morning Miss Bentley, good morning every-one,' they chanted.

'Don't you all look wonderful this morning,' she said, scanning the rows of children who gazed back with expectant, happy faces. 'Everyone looks really, really super. My goodness, what a lot of different characters we have in the hall today. It's going to be really hard to judge which of you are the best, so I have asked two of my friends to help me. I think you all know Mrs Arkwright' – she indicated the Chairman of Governors sitting at the side – 'and some of you may remember Mr Phinn who visited our school last year. Well, Mr Phinn is going to take our assembly this morning and then help us decide which of you are the most imaginatively dressed characters. Over to you, Mr Phinn.'

I had decided that I would read the children the parable of the lost sheep. It's a short account and I thought it would be very appropriate for an assembly and would relate to the children, many of whom came from farming backgrounds.

'Good morning, children,' I said, moving to the front of the hall. 'Today, as you know, is Children's Reading Day and Miss Bentley has asked me to talk to you about some of my favourite books.' I held up a large crimson-coloured volume, on the front of which the title, *Stories from the Bible*, was picked out in large golden lettering. 'This book was given to me by my mother many years ago when I was a little boy. It is a very special book, full of wonderful stories which were told by a very special man. Does anyone know who I mean?'

'Jesus,' chorused the children.

'Yes, it's Jesus, and although Jesus never wrote down any of his stories, his friends did, and millions of people have read what he said nearly two thousand years ago. Jesus wanted everyone to be kind and love each other and was often surrounded by people who did not have much money, people who had done wrong, people who had got into trouble, people who were sick and lonely. In this story, which is called "The Story of the Lost Sheep", Jesus tries to help us understand how we should feel about the poor and weak.'

Every eye was on me as I read the story. 'Imagine that a shepherd had a hundred sheep. One day, when he counted them, he found that there was one missing. He could have said, "Well, it's only one missing, I've got ninety-nine more. I won't bother looking for it." But he didn't say that. He left all the other sheep untended and went in search of the one lost sheep until he found it. Now why do you think he did that?' I hoped that the children would appreciate the meaning of the parable, that every single one of us is valuable in the eyes of God and that 'there is more joy in heaven when one sinner turns back to God than ninety-nine who see no need to repent'. But the point was missed.

'Why do you think the shepherd risked losing all the other sheep just for the one which was lost?' I asked again.

A thoughtful-looking little boy on the front row raised a hand. ''Appen it were t'tup!' he said.

Not the answer I had been hoping for. I pressed on, explaining what parables were and how they taught us all how to lead better lives. I could see by the fidgeting and turning of heads that I was not having a massive impact on the children who were obviously keen to get on with the judging of the costumes, so I decided to finish. But not before posing one final question.

'And what would you say to Jesus,' I asked, holding

high the red book like some preacher of old, 'if he were to walk into the hall this morning?'

The boy on the front row thought for a moment, then raised his hand a second time and said loudly, 'I'd give 'im that book, Mester Phinn, and I'd say, "Jesus Christ – this is your life!"'

The judging of the competition went a great deal better. Before us paraded a whole host of book characters: Long John Silver and Peter Rabbit, Paddington Bear and Peter Pan, Robin Hood and Cinderella. Last of all came a pathetic-looking little boy in wrinkled yellow tights, electric-blue underpants and a T-shirt with SUPAMAN written incorrectly across the front. I heard a few suppressed giggles and whispers from the other children and saw their smirks and smiles.

Mrs Arkwright and I awarded the first prize to the Little Mermaid, the second prize to Aladdin and the third prize to a very pleased little boy in yellow tights, electric-blue underpants and a T-shirt with SUPAMAN written incorrectly across the front. He scampered out to the front of the hall, his weeping and whimpering ceased and the frowns were replaced by a great beaming smile.

I said my farewells to the children and Mrs Arkwright and headed for the door. Christine followed me and when she had made sure we were out of sight of everyone slipped her hand through my arm.

'That was really nice of you,' she said, giving me a quick peck on the cheek and then rubbing out the greenish smear that had been left behind. 'Gavin won't stop talking about that for weeks. You're an old softie really, aren't you?'

'Maybe, but I think the assembly was a bit over their heads,' I said.

'Um, yes, just a bit. I've got to go. But will you ring me? We could have an evening together.'

A large, round-faced boy appeared from the hall. He wore a bright red blouse, baggy blue pants, large red floppy hat with a small silver bell on the end and huge black shoes. His lips were crimson, his eyes lined in thick black mascara and two scarlet circles adorned each cheek. It was a grotesque parody of Noddy.

'Mr Phinn! Mr Phinn!' he gabbled. 'I need one of those pieces of paper which you gave to Gavin which says I don't look a prat.'

6

Connie, the caretaker of the Staff Development Centre, was a good-hearted, down-to-earth Yorkshire woman with an acerbic wit and wonderful command of the most inventive malapropisms and *non sequiturs*. She had no conception of rank, status or position and treated everyone exactly the same – with a bluntness bordering on the rude. If the Pope himself were to pay a visit to the Staff Development Centre and make use of the washroom facilities, Connie would no doubt have detained His Holiness as he departed, with the words: 'I hope you've left them Gents as you found them!' Were the

Queen to grace the portals of the SDC, Connie would have no compunction in telling Her Majesty to wipe her feet before entering and to return her cup to the serving hatch after use. Should the Prime Minister enter the building, Connie would have not the slightest hesitation in asking the right honourable gentleman if he had parked his car well away from the front doors because blocking her entrance was a health-and-safety hazard. It was unthinkable that she was at the end of any chain of command, that she could be directed to carry out instructions or, perish the thought, be given such a thing as an order. It was Connie who was at the controls when people were on her territory.

Connie could be quite unnerving. Teachers attending courses at the Centre would be listening to a speaker and, glancing up, would see Connie's round, florid face grimacing at the door. During the coffee-break, they would find an ample woman with a bright copper-coloured perm and dressed in a pink nylon overall hovering in the background, usually surveying them with a malevolent expression. At lunchtime they would be eating their sandwiches nervously, making certain not a crumb fell on the spotless carpet, sensing that small sharp eyes, like those of a blackbird searching for a worm, were watching from behind the serving hatch. When, at the end of the day, the equipment had been put neatly away, the chairs carefully stacked, the rooms left in an orderly fashion, litter placed in the appropriate receptacles and all crockery returned to the kitchen, Connie would stride around her empire, feather duster held like a field-marshal's baton, her nylon overall crackling, to make sure that everything was left as it had been found earlier that day. And woe-betide anyone who flouted these unwritten rules.

The Staff Development Centre, where all the courses and conferences for teachers and most of the staff interviews took place, was a tribute to Connie's hard work and dedication. She scrubbed and scoured, polished and dusted, mopped and wiped with a vengeance. The building, inside and out, was always immaculately clean and tidy, not a speck of dusk or a scuffmark was to be seen anywhere and it always smelt of lavender furniture polish and carbolic soap. The toilets were her pride and joy. The porcelain sparkled and the floors gleamed. The Staff Development Centre was Connie's palace.

If any one of us was ever inclined to suggest to her that she should show a little more deference and respect, that person would desist, knowing that deep down this woman had a heart of gold and that no one could do the job better than she. Everyone who knew her was prepared to tolerate her abrupt manner and sharp tongue for those very reasons. Everyone, that is, except Sidney Clamp. Sidney – noisy, unpredictable, untidy, madly creative – was guaranteed to ruffle the feathers of her duster and wind Connie up to distraction.

I arrived at the SDC one dull Friday afternoon to prepare for an English course I was to direct the following Monday. In the entrance hall stood Connie, in fierce and heated discussion with Sidney. She was dressed, as usual, in her pink nylon overall and was clutching her feather duster magisterially.

'Look here, Connie,' Sidney was trying to explain to her, 'you have to accept a bit of a mess. For goodness sake, it was an *art* course. Art is not like mathematics, you know, it's not orderly, it's not methodical, it's not tidy. We artists need to use messy materials like paints, charcoals, crayons, clay, cardboard and glue.' He waved his hands about theatrically as though conducting some invisible orchestra. 'People have to express themselves in art, be creative, imaginative and they are therefore often untidy. It's par for the course.'

Connie pulled one of her many expressions of distaste, the face of someone suffering from acute indigestion. 'Well, it's not part of *my* course, Mr Clamp,' she retorted, 'and I don't want these artists, as you call them, expressing themselves like that in *my* Centre. They can clear up after themselves. They do have hands, I take it, if they are doing all these creative carryings on. Then they can use those hands to clear up and they don't need to leave a trail of debris and destruction behind like what they have this afternoon.'

'Hardly a trail of debris and destruction,' sighed Sidney.

'Oh, yes, they did, Mr Clamp, and I can't be doing with it.'

Sidney continued to wave his hands about elaborately. 'Einstein said that genius is seldom tidy.'

'I don't care what Einstein or any of your other artificated friends have to say. I am not cleaning up that mess and that's that. It's all very well for you and this

Einstein to leave the room as if a bomb has hit it, I'm the one left to pick up the pieces. I'm telling you, I don't intend picking up the mess that you've left today. It's just not fair to expect me to do it, Mr Clamp.'

'First of all, Connie,' said Sidney, 'Einstein is dead.'

'Well, I'm very sorry to hear it, I'm sure, but that's no excuse for the mess that was left in that room. It was spotless when you went in this morning, you could have eaten your dinner off of that floor, and now look at it! Anyway,' she said, running her feather duster along a window ledge, 'it's my bingo night and I'm not missing the first house just because I have to stop here to clear up.'

'Good afternoon,' I said in a loud and cheerful voice, determined to get their attention since until then neither seemed to have noticed me.

'Hello, Gervase,' moaned Sidney.

'Good afternoon,' said Connie through tight little lips. 'Anyhow, I've said what I had to say, Mr Clamp, and I insist that you will see that that room is left as you found it before you go. I could let this Centre go to rack and ruin but I keep it nice and tidy.'

'I know you do, Connie,' began Sidney.

'It's no skin off my feet if it was just left but you'd be soon complaining if you found the room like that at the *start* of your course.'

'Very well, Connie,' Sidney told her, bowing with a flourish. 'I give in. I surrender. I yield. I shall remain behind and return the art room to its pristine splendour and perhaps my kind and obliging colleague here will lend a helpful hand.'

'Certainly not!' I spluttered. 'I'm sorry, Sidney, but I have a course to prepare and then I'm meeting Christine at Mama's Pizza Parlour. You're on your own.'

'What happened to friendship and camaraderie?' asked Sidney to no one in particular. 'Whither went the Good Samaritan?'

'He probably didn't have a date and it wasn't his bingo night,' I replied flippantly.

'Very droll,' said Sidney.

'Well, just so long as it gets done,' came Connie's final riposte before she marched off down the corridor, flicking the feather duster at invisible dust and crackling as she went.

'That woman,' said Sidney through clamped teeth, 'will drive me to drink.'

'Speaking of drink,' I said, 'I'll see if I can get Connie to rustle you up a cup of tea before you start on the art room. You might be there some time.'

'She'll probably put toilet bleach in it if she knows the tea's for me, and considering the mood I'm in at the moment, I would most probably drink it. But, come on, Gervase,' he pleaded, 'lend a hand, please, there's a good fellow.'

'I'm sorry, Sidney, but I can't. I just don't have the time.'

'That most foul dragon in pink will be watching my every move.'

'Don't judge her too harshly,' I said. 'Her heart's in the right place.'

'The right place for Connie's heart, dear boy,' replied

Sidney, summoning up a faint smile, 'is on the end of a stake.' With that he departed for the art room.

Having checked the equipment in the English room, set out the chairs, displayed a range of books and materials and put a programme on each table, I headed for the kitchen. By this time Sidney, who had made a half-hearted attempt to clear up the mess in the art room, had crept away. Connie was vigorously wiping the Formica top on the serving hatch.

'Right, that's sorted,' I told her.

'I hope the art room is,' she snapped. 'That Mr Clamp will drive me to drink. I don't know how you can share an office with him. I've never met anyone so untidy. And that Mr Pritchard is not a whole lot better, forever leaving his equipment all over the place. Anyway, have you got everything you need for Monday?' she asked.

'Yes, all ready and prepared.'

'I put some extra paper on the flip chart.'

'That's very good of you.'

'And I've put out some more felt tip markers. I know how you like to write.'

'Thank you, Connie.'

'Do you want a cup of tea?'

I glanced at my watch. I was not intending to go home before meeting Christine so had a bit of time to kill. 'Yes, thanks.'

As Connie clanked and clattered in the cupboard behind the hatch, I had visions of her and Sidney, having driven each other to drink, ending up in the same drying-out clinic. Not a happy thought, and I pushed it from my wicked mind.

'I'm getting married, you know,' I said, accepting the proffered mug

'You're not, are you?' she gasped. 'Is it that nice young woman with the blonde hair, Miss Bentley?'

'Well, it's not likely to be anyone else, Connie, is it?' I laughed. 'I'm not exactly your Casanova.'

'Well, you never know,' she said, starting to pour her tea again. 'You seem to be very pally with that little nun. That Sister Brenda.'

'Sister Brendan.'

'That's her. You seem to hit it off with her and no mistake. She's forever on your courses.'

'Nuns are celibate, Connie,' I told her.

'They're celi-what?'

'They're not allowed to get married.'

'Yes, well, as I've said to you before, I had no idea she was a nun when I first met her. I was talking to her as if she was a normal person. There was no long black skirt or headgear. I didn't know she was a nun. She looked like an air hostess in that dark blue suit and with her hair all buffeted up. If they can drive cars and dress like that, I reckon it won't be long before they're getting married. Anyway, I hope you and Miss Bentley will be very happy.'

'Thanks, Connie.'

'You've not known her that long, have you? In my day, we used to walk out together for a few years before we decided to get married. I think the reason for all the divorces these days is that people rush into it.'

'I've been going out with Christine for nearly two years.'

'That doesn't mean a thing. No, gone are the days of long courtships and chaperones and getting engaged and asking fathers for their daughter's hand. These days, most people don't seem to bother with marriage. They "live over the brush", as my mother would say. They don't have husbands and wives nowadays, they have partners. I ask you! That's what you have on the dance floor, a partner. You wonder what the world's coming to, don't you? Take my cousin's girl. She's at West Challerton High, supposed to be doing her exams this year. She changes her boyfriends as often as she changes her knickers.'

It was definitely time for me to go.

7

The last day of term was an emotional occasion. I had been invited to Winnery Nook Nursery and Infants School to be introduced to the children not as the school inspector but as Miss Bentley's future husband and for a presentation from the governors, staff and children. One small boy in particular touched our hearts.

Barry was six and it was clear to everyone who met him that he was a neglected child who desperately sought affection. His shirt was invariably dirty, his trousers frayed, his jumper spattered in stains and he had that unpleasant, unwashed smell about him.

'He's from a large one-parent family,' Christine had told me, when I had met the little boy on a previous visit to the school. 'I don't suppose he gets much attention at home. His mother is a sharp-tongued, miserable woman and, from what I gather, finds it difficult to cope. Demanding young children, too little money, mounting debts, absentee father – or, more likely, fathers – a string of violent boyfriends. It's perhaps no surprise that she looks permanently exhausted and that she flies off the handle at every opportunity. But Barry deserves better. She seems to have no interest in him at all.'

'What a life,' I had said.

Despite his background, Barry was a remarkably cheerful little boy who never complained and always tried his limited best at his schoolwork. 'Hello, Miss Bentley,' he would shout brightly each morning as he waited for her at the entrance to the school. 'Any jobs, miss?' He loved nothing better than to straighten the chairs, give out the paper and pencils, collect the books, tidy up the classroom and pick up litter, whistling away whilst doing these tasks as if he had not a care in the world.

It was just after the assembly on this final morning, where we had been presented with a large box wrapped in silvery wedding paper and festooned with ribbons and silver horseshoes, when Barry appeared. Some of the children had brought individual presents and cards, others had arrived at school with great bunches of daffodils, tulips and other spring flowers. Soon we were surrounded by a chattering, excited throng of children, all eager to wish us well. Barry had held back until Christine and I had begun to make our way to her office.

'Hello, Barry,' Christine said, catching sight of him lingering in the corridor. 'Come along and meet my fiancé. Do you remember Mr Phinn?'

The little boy surveyed me seriously. He was carrying two small branches of faded broom which had seen better days and a couple of forlorn irises, wrapped in a piece of colourful paper which I realised was a page torn out of a magazine.

'Are you really getting married, miss?' he asked sadly.

'Yes, I am,' Christine replied, crouching down so she was on his level. She took his grubby little hand in hers. 'Aren't you going to say "hello" to my husband-to-be?'

'Hello,' the little boy mumbled disconsolately.

'Hello, Barry,' I replied.

'And next term I'll be Mrs Phinn,' Christine told him. 'Isn't it exciting?'

'I like you as Miss Bentley,' he said unhappily. 'I don't want you getting married. I don't want you to. I don't, I don't!' And he burst into tears.

'I'll still be the same person, Barry. I won't be any different.'

'You will! You will!' he wailed piteously. 'I know you will.' Then he looked up at Christine, sniffing and sobbing and rubbing his eyes. '*I* wanted to marry you.'

Christine wrapped her arms around his small shaking body. 'And are these lovely flowers for me?' she asked in a trembling voice. I knew she was as affected by this pathetic little scene as I was. He gave a little nod. 'They're beautiful, and I shall put them in water and have them on my desk. These shall be my very special flowers.'

She took his hand, led him into the staff room, and found the most colourful vase from under the sink. The flowers were arranged and we followed Christine back to her office where she had put the vase in pride of place on her desk. She gave the little boy a hug. 'These are my very special flowers, Barry. Thank you so much. I like them better than any other flowers I have been given.'

Chris told me later that, at the end of the day, the little boy had appeared at her door.

'Hello, Barry,' she had said brightly. 'Have you come to wish me all the best for my wedding next week?'

'I've come for my flowers, miss,' he had said bluntly.

'Your flowers? Oh, I thought they were for me.'

'They're very special,' the child had said solemnly. 'You said they were very special.'

'And they are,' Christine had told him. 'I think they are beautiful but I thought you brought them for me.'

'They're very special,' Barry had repeated, 'and I want to give them to my mam.'

Christine had smiled. 'Of course, you do.' She had removed the broom, virtually bare of its yellow blossom, and the two wilting irises from the vase and had wrapped them in some bright red tissue paper. Then, taking a ribbon from one of the wedding presents, she had tied them in a bunch. 'They look really nice now, don't they?' she had said. 'What a lovely surprise for your mummy.' Christine had placed the flowers in the child's hands. 'But do you think I might have just a little sprig of broom for good luck? I'll put it with my bouquet when I get married.' The child had nodded and snapped a sprig from a branch.

Christine had watched Barry scurry down the school path to be met at the gates by a stocky, unkempt woman with short bleached hair and a cigarette dangling from her mouth. Two screaming toddlers were writhing and wriggling in the push-chair beside her. On seeing her son, she had stabbed the air with a finger and had begun shouting at him. Reaching her, the little boy had held up his bouquet like a priest at the altar making an offering. The flowers had been promptly plucked from his hand and deposited in the nearest bin.

'What a life,' I had said to Christine when she told me this, 'what a life!'

8

The last lesson of the day at King Henry's College was with the sixth form and a newly qualified teacher. I arrived at the rather noisy classroom to find twenty or so students sitting around tables in animated discussion.

'Is there a teacher here?' I asked, raising my voice above the hubbub.

'I'm the teacher,' replied one young man sitting near the door, giving me a broad smile. 'Simon Purdey.'

'Oh, I'm sorry, Mr Purdey,' I said. 'I thought you were one of the students.'

'Well, there's only a few years between us and I've been told that I look young for my age. You must be Mr Fish, the inspector.'

'Phinn,' I corrected.

'Oh, I did wonder when we were told it was Fish. Sounded a bit suspicious.'

'What are the students doing this afternoon?' I inquired.

'We're studying *Hamlet* as our "A" level text and I've asked the students to read through Act 1 and re-write it in a different genre: as a modern radio play, the opening chapter of a detective novel, a horror story, thriller, romance, monologue, documentary drama, that sort of thing. Each group has a different genre to consider.'

'Sounds interesting,' I said.

'Well, I thought it would get them straight into the play and also be a bit of fun before we start the more serious business of looking at the actual text. I think it's a better way than wading drearily through Shakespeare as I did at school. Do you know, we were made to write out passages of Shakespeare as a punishment? Would you credit that? The greatest words in the English language and they were set as a punishment! I only really came to appreciate Shakespeare when I was in the sixth form and a new teacher arrived. She just turned me on.'

'Yes,' I said, 'I had a remarkable English teacher in the sixth form, too.'

'Anyway,' continued the young man, 'I thought that by writing the opening of the play in another form, the students would have to read the first act carefully and critically and then transpose it, making decisions about what to include and what to omit. Later we will look at the actual text itself, act it out. Do you want to see how far they have got?'

'Yes, I would,' I replied.

As I watched the series of highly original openings being acted out in front of the rest of the class, I recalled my sixth-form years when I too studied Shakespeare's most famous play. I was taught by a Miss Wainwright, a small, softly spoken woman who invariably wore a pristine white blouse buttoned up at the neck and a long dark skirt. The small lace handkerchief that she secreted up her sleeve would be occasionally plucked out to dab her mouth. Save for the large cameo brooch placed at her throat, she wore no jewellery and there was no vestige of make-up. What were so memorable about this remarkable teacher were her eyes. They shone with intensity, especially when she was discussing her favourite subject, Shakespeare.

She had taken us to see a production of *King Lear* at the Rotherham Civic Theatre. I realise now that the acting had been wooden and the costumes bizarre, but the beauty and poignancy of the language had come through. King Lear had entered with his dead daughter draped in his arms and he howling to the heavens: 'She is gone forever!' To my horror, Miss Wainwright – sitting one away from me in the row – had begun to cry, and I was soon doing the same. She had indeed been an amazing teacher.

Whenever I saw an outstanding English teacher, I often thought of Miss Mary Wainwright and thanked God for the good fortune of having been taught by her.

My thoughts were interrupted when I heard my name mentioned by the teacher. 'And the last version is one that Mr Phinn, as a Yorkshireman, will appreciate. It's the Yorkshire version of *Hamlet*.'

Two boys, ambled towards each other at the front of the room, hands thrust deep in their pockets.

'Hey up, 'Amlet.'

'Hey up, 'Oratio, what's tha doin' 'ere?'

'Nowt much. 'Ow abaat thee then, 'Amlet? I ant seen thee for a bit.'

'Nay, I'm not that champion, 'Oratio, if t'truth be towld.'

'Whay, 'Amlet, what's oop?'

'Mi dad's deead, mi mam's married mi uncle and mi girlfriend does nowt but nag, nag, nag. I tell thee, 'Oratio, I'm weary wi' it.'

'Aye, tha's not far wrong theer, 'Amlet, She's gor a reight gob on 'er, that Hophilia. Teks after 'er owld man.'

'Anyroad, 'Oratio, what's tha doin 'ere in Helsinor?'

'I've come for thee dad's funeral.'

'More like mi mam's wedding.'

'Aye, she dint let t'grass grow under 'er feet, did she?'

'I don't know what mi owld man 'ud mek of it, 'Oratio, I really don't.'

'Well, tha can ask 'im theeself, 'Amlet.'

''Ow's tha mean?'

''E's been walkin' on t'battlements every neet this

week, a-mooanin' and a-grooanin' and purrin' t'wind up iverybody. We're sick to deeath on it, 'Amlet, we really are.'

'Ger on!'

'It's reight, 'Amlet. 'E won't shurrup. A-mooanin' and a-grooanin an' a-clankin' abaat like there's no tomorra.'

'I wonder wor 'e wants?'

'Well, tha can ask 'im thaself, cos 'ere 'e comes now.'

A third boy entered. ''Ey up, our 'Amlet.'

''Ey up, Dad. How's it gooin'?'

''Ow's it gooin'? How's it gooin'? What's tha mean, how's it gooin'? I'm deead, 'Amlet, and I'm not that chuffed abaat it.'

'Oh, aye, I forgot.'

'I was done in, 'Amlet, murdered, killed, slayed, bumped off, hassassinated.'

'Ee, that were a rotten trick.'

'Rotten trick! Rotten trick! It were bloody criminal, that's what it were.'

'Who did it, Dad?'

'Mi kid brother.'

'Mi Uncle Claudius?'

'Aye, 'im what's nicked mi crown and married thee mam.'

'What's to do, then, Dad?'

'What's tha mean, what's to do?'

'What's tha come back fer?'

'I wants thee to sooart thy uncle out, that's what I wants thee to do. I wants thee to do to 'im what 'e did to me, our 'Amlet. Now I 'ope tha's got t'gumption for it. Come on, 'Oratio, let's let t'lad get crackin'. '

As I watched and laughed along with the teacher and students, I thought of Miss Wainwright's words that young people are naturally very funny. She was right: humour is highly related to learning and adds inestimably to our quality of life. There are few things more pleasurable to hear in life than young people laughing unselfconsciously.

Following the performance, there was loud and spontaneous applause and cheering which died suddenly when the door opened and there stood the Headteacher, Mr Frobisher, like 'The Ghost of Christmas Past'.

'There is a great deal of noise coming from this room,' he said. 'I could hear it at the end of the corridor.'

'We're studying *Hamlet*,' explained Mr Purdey, seemingly unperturbed by the interruption.

'Really? I wasn't aware, Mr Purdey, that *Hamlet* was quite so amusing,' he said without a glimmer of a smile, and left the room.

I thought back to Miss Wainwright who had taught me English and, above all, to appreciate the works of Shakespeare. She had brought the Bard to life, and developed in me a love of literature for which I shall be forever grateful. She, I knew, would have loved the version of *Hamlet* we had just seen, and would have laughed along with the rest of us.

POCKET PENGUINS

POCKET PENGUINS